FULFILLING GOD'S PURPOSE

A 30-Day
Devotional To Enhance The Discovery
and Fulfillment of Your Purpose

By
Apostle L'Tanya C. Perry, MDiv.

TRAINING WITH APOSTLE PERRY

Note: In English usage, the word satan should be capitalized because it is a proper noun. However, I refuse to capitalize the word 'satan' as it gives satan undue "status."

Paperback ISBN-978-1-957052-27-4
E-book ISBN-978-1-957052-28-1

Printed in the United States of America.

TAP Press

TAP Press Publishing
PO BOX 561
Granite Falls, NC 28630

DEDICATION

I thank God for placing me on the earth to fulfill His grand purpose. Furthermore, I am grateful to God for giving me as a gift to my mom. She was exceptional support towards the fulfillment of my purpose. She gave her time, energy, resources, and prayers, to see me become who God created me to be.

I also dedicate this book to NBWC citizens for staying the course. No matter how it looks, God called us to build a work that will outlive us. Always remember God's Word in Romans 8:28 (KJV), *"All things work together for the good for those who love the Lord and called to His purpose."*

I acknowledge the TAP team. Everyone around the world whom God has divinely appointed to partner with me to fulfill my writing and teaching purpose. God will use any willing vessel. I'm so honored to work with all of you.

And to my husband, Kelvin, Alexus, KJ, and my grand-doggie Blue. You all played a significant role, standing by me as I live out my God-given assignment. I know it wasn't easy on you all, but you see the fruit of our labor in our given areas. Know that God is still making and molding us.

Stay the course!!!

CONTENTS

DAY 1
HOW DO YOU MEASURE SUCCESS?

Scriptural Text: *"Charge them that are rich in this world, that they be not high-minded, nor trust in uncertain riches, but in the living God, who giveth us richly all things to enjoy; That they do good, that they be rich in good works, ready to distribute, willing to communicate;"*

–1 Timothy 6:17-18 KJV

Inspiring Commentary

In our world today, it seems awkward our checklists for defining success. We draw our definitions from all the externals. But the true measure of success goes beyond increasing your Net worth or becoming the new richest man on earth. It goes beyond building a house beside the beach and walking down the driveway every morning to have a feel of the beauty of nature. Success in life, I believe, starts with providing intelligible answers to the existential questions of life. Hence, the discovery of purpose here on earth is a catalyst to true and lasting success.

On the 15th of September 2020, the Forbes Daily cover carried an absorbing headline about Chuck Feeney—a philanthropist: "THE BILLIONAIRE WHO WANTED TO DIE BROKE...IS NOW OFFICIALLY BROKE."[1] Wow, unbelievable! Does that sound like what an average American would wish for? Who in the world ever desires to die broke? So, what was the big gist? Forbes writes, *"It took decades, but Chuck Feeney, the former billionaire cofounder of retail giant Duty Free Shoppers has finally given all his money away to charity. He has nothing left now—and he couldn't be happier."*[2]

Vince Lombardi, a Football Player and Coach once said, *"Success demands singleness of purpose."*[3] For Feeney, what defines success isn't having a million dollars in his bank account while others have nothing. Over four decades, Feeney donated more than $8 billion to charities, universities, and foundations worldwide through his foundation—*The Atlantic Philanthropies. "We learned a lot. We would do some things differently, but I am very satisfied. I feel very good about completing this on my watch. My thanks to all who joined us on this journey. And to those wondering about Giving While Living: Try it, you'll like it,"* Feeney tells Forbes.[4]

Ordinarily, finding meaning, and asking the existential question, *"Why are we here?"* is essential to living a fulfilled life. But we have misunderstood it to mean a pursuit of stereotypical and manmade standards of success. Indeed, success is a buzzword in our world today. Everybody wants it, and some will stop at nothing to achieve it. However, behind the success craze is a desire for fulfillment. This desire is found in every human being. It makes us restless and itches for something more than just existing. To ease that restlessness and scratch that itch in the soul, we engage in the pursuit of happiness.

Many people have pursued success believing that it was the way to happiness. Others have risked and sacrificed other areas of their lives for business and career success. They believed that fame and money would solve all their problems. Maybe if they had all the money they needed, their lives would be better, fuller, richer. But unfortunately, the reverse was the case. According to the world's standards, the more successful they were, the more dissatisfied they became. So, seek a life of fulfillment, seek to live a life of impact, and endeavour to love people around you genuinely, and that's the true measure of success. Success is not amassing wealth but fulfillment in your area of calling. Let this be your goal always.

Call to Action

How do you describe success, and what's your definition of a successful person?

____

____

____

____

____

List three achievements you are aiming for in life that will make you happy.

____

____

____

____

____

Prayer

Father, in the name of Jesus, I thank You for the truth of your word today. I pray that You help me to measure success according to Your pattern. Help me by Your Spirit not to limit my life to the world's standard, but I pray for the grace to always do good and be a light to the world. In Jesus' name. Amen.

DAY 2
WHEN DOES LIFE BEGIN?

Scriptural Text: *"Before I formed thee in the belly I knew thee; and before thou camest forth out of the womb I sanctified thee, and I ordained thee a prophet unto the nations."*

–Jeremiah 1:5 KJV

Inspiring Commentary

When does life really begin? For instance, during the nine months of a baby's development in the womb, did you know that some people retain the pronoun "*it*" for the baby until birth? Usually, this saves us from the complexities of rightly placing the child's identity or gender. Babies aren't objects. They have life and all the characteristics an adult possesses, but life of purpose on the earth begins for babies the day they are welcomed to this world.

Many wake up every morning driven by the *American Dream*. Just scouting every possible means or opportunity for prosperity and success. To measure up to the *American Dream* and make ends meet, many hold two or more jobs and work overtime if need be. With the myriad of pros that come with this, we seem cool with it once money keeps coming in. With this mindset, the purpose of life has taken a different rhythm because of our drive to make it big.

While I have nothing against the concept behind the Declaration of Independence that made for the equality of man, right to life, liberty, and pursuit of happiness, it only seems that many have been damaged over the years by this vague pursuit than helped. As a result, they end their lives in regret of never fulfilling a dream they weren't even fashioned to fulfill in the first place.

Think about a fish dreaming of flying someday; that will never happen. This is because fishes' liberty, comfort, and satisfaction are derived from swimming—not flying. So likewise, a man is truly living when he understands the correct habitat that defines his possibilities. That is, when you wake up from bed every morning to pursue what gives you a sense of divine purpose, assignment, fulfillment and satisfaction. Dr Myles Munroe once said, *"The greatest tragedy in life is not death, but a life without a purpose."*[5] By implication, living without a purpose is more tragic than death. It would be better to never have existed than live a wasted life. Friend, you should understand that just as a fetus in the womb without a definite identity, you have no identity; neither are you living until you can conceive your purpose. Without purpose, life becomes a burden.

Purpose is the reason for which something exists or is done, made, or used.[6] It is an intended or desired result, aim, or goal. We are on earth for a reason. We didn't evolve by chance from plants or lower organisms. You were created to achieve God's desired result. If you read today's text again, the Scripture shows that God has a map of your life. He knew exactly what He was forming even before creating you. Your life isn't coincidental: it is intentional. Are you wondering if your life is intentional? The answer is yes. Why? Because God had an intention for your existence. Hence, the earlier you know this truth, the wiser you get in pursuing the discovery of your purpose.

Call to Action

What is your view about the importance of purpose in life.

Have you discovered your purpose on earth? Could you describe it in words?

Prayer

Father, in the name of Jesus, I thank You because I am not a non-entity. I thank You because You didn't just dump me mindlessly on the earth; rather, You were deliberate about my creation. I pray that You open the eyes of my heart wider to my purpose on the earth. I pray that You will help me to further discover and live up to Your expectation for my life. In Jesus' name. Amen.

DAY 3
TURN WITHIN

Scriptural Text: *"I praise you, for I am fearfully and wonderfully made. Wonderful are your works; my soul knows it very well."*

–Psalms 139:14 ESV

Inspiring Commentary

We are in a time where seeking validation from people is a norm. Society defines for us what beauty is, what is ugly, and what things to possess to be tagged among the successful class. The world tries to define people by their limitations and set expectations, which, if not met, automatically lead to rejection. Maybe it's part of our human nature to label, divide, or organize into categories. But the big problem is we forget that even though we're equal, we have uniqueness and have a different spectrum of strengths.

Some never believe they're beautiful until they get some validation from others. Today, just a word of criticism could be the trigger to committing suicide. Living within the bubble of societal expectations will surely hamper your divine possibilities, uniqueness, and purpose. Understand that your purpose isn't a function of who or what people, circumstances, and experiences have defined you.

It's tough for people to understand their purpose today because they keep turning to the wrong sources. No person matures, praying to see all their biological makeups develop. They don't look externally for all their characteristics to develop—they're put there from the day they were born. The same applies to purpose. No one gets to know who they are by looking for it within the things of the world. You must turn your eyes off all the challenges, limitations, rejections, as well as life's uncertainties and see the precious gift God has hidden within you to bless the world.

Too often, we find ourselves replaying the role of the widow of Zarephath in Scriptures, who thinks a little oil is nothing. Or Moses, who never knew the rod in his hands would be instrumental to some of the greatest miracles in Bible history. More often than not, the root of our suffering and confusion about purpose is that we scorn what God has gifted us. However, if we turn within and take a break from what people say, we'll soon discover the vast island of resources in us that are yet untapped. But when we live this way, we become deaf to the noise of life and society. We are then left with a deep understanding and thankfulness for who God has made us to be-which is wonderful and precious.

In Exodus 4:1-2 (KJV), the Bible says, *"And Moses answered and said, But, behold, they will not believe me, nor hearken unto my voice: for they will say, The LORD hath not appeared unto thee. And the LORD said unto him, What is that in thine hand? And he said, A rod."* In this passage, Moses couldn't see much about his life because he was looking at the circumstances surrounding his birth and his exile. Now it seems like the purpose in his heart is just a mirage. But God told him to look within. Look at what is in your hand. Remember, he has always held the same rod for the past forty years leading and guiding the sheep; meanwhile, it was an instrument for the fulfillment of his assignment. God had to turn his face within. You are loaded with all that you need to shine in life. Nothing will be imported; rather, you only need to look within and discover what you have probably always ignored.

Like Adam, you were designed to reveal God's glory through your nature, character and influence your environment. In the general mandate to have dominion resides your personal mandate. God wants you to have a particular kind of influence in a given field. So, you have a responsibility to discover it. That's your purpose: God's desire for your life.

Call to Action

Describe three things you can do perfectly but aren't paying much attention to.

____

____

____

____

____

Prayer

Father, in the name of Jesus, I thank You for the insight from Your Word today. I pray that You open my eyes to what You have deposited in me. I pray that I will no longer despise Your grace and calling upon my life, but You will help me to stir it and fan it to flame. Like Moses, I shall see signs through the blessings of God in my life. In Jesus' name. Amen.

DAY 4

YOUR LIFE IS DELIBERATE

Scriptural Text: *"I will praise thee; for I am fearfully and wonderfully made: marvellous are Thy works; and that my soul knoweth right well."*

–Psalm 139:14 KJV

Inspiring Commentary

How did the world come to be? Who knew the beginning and what was in the beginning before the beginning even began. What is the origin of man? What was in existence before the earth and man came to be? Has any of these questions ever crossed your mind recently?

It is to solve this puzzling question of the origin of man and, by extension, the earth that scholars through the ages have postulated pretty intellectual and wild theories to this effect. Amidst several theories, scientists, astronomers, and cosmologists seem to agree and reach a consensus that the universe was created in a massive explosion. Can you imagine that? How can something as structured as the earth come out of destruction? Think about it.

While these thoughts and conclusions seem convincing to the learned, the book of Genesis brings to light the true beginning of creation. The Bible shows that human beings aren't a result of an explosion or a thoughtless beginning. We are a product of an intelligent and careful craft of the all-powerful being—God! Many Christian Scholars believe the Bible isn't just a spiritual or inspired piece but a historical document with several shreds of evidence to prove its authenticity. It is to this effect that I'll like to draw from what the Bible says about our origin.

According to Genesis 1:1-2 (KJV), the Bible says, *"In the beginning God created the heaven and the earth. And the earth was without form, and void; and darkness was upon the face of the deep. And the Spirit of God moved upon the face of the waters."* From this account, it proves that God is the mastermind behind creation—not an explosion. To further probe the Biblical shreds of evidence of creation, Genesis 2:7-8 (KJV) says, *"And the LORD God formed man of the dust of the ground, and breathed into his nostrils the breath of life; and man became a living soul. And the LORD God planted a garden eastward in Eden; and there he put the man whom he had formed."*

From the passages above, we see the grand designer of the universe and how He placed man within it. If we allow the fallen man to arrogantly theorize and define God out of our consciousness, we'll forever live for the mundane. Purpose begins with discovering the Maker of all things and being responsible to Him.

The end of living a meaningless life begins with the discovery of purpose. First, you must believe that you're not on the earth by accident; rather, your life is deliberate. God had a purpose for creating you and sent you to the earth to fulfill that purpose. That purpose is why you're alive: your preoccupation as long as you live. So, take your mind off any other idea that takes God out of the foundation of your existence. Psalm 139:14 says you were fearfully created by no other but the Almighty.

Call to Action

List three things that you are confident are special about you.

____

____

____

____

____

Prayer

Father, in the name of Jesus, I thank You for the careful thought of creating me. I thank You because I am carefully and gorgeously made. I thank You because I am not an error trying to be made right; rather, I am a masterpiece of the Most High. Therefore, Father, help me to live in this reality all the days of my life. In Jesus' name. Amen.

DAY 5
MEET THE MANUFACTURER

Scriptura Text: *"I alone know the plans I have for you, plans to bring you prosperity and not disaster, plans to bring about the future you hope for."*
–Jeremiah 29:11 GNB

Inspiring Commentary

When was the last time you purchase a new gadget? Did you care to read the user manual? Let's face it, many users of new products don't bother to read the manual. Maybe we always feel we have the know-how at our fingertips, or we feel we're too busy to sit with a little booklet full of instructions, guidelines, and some troubleshooting steps to operating a gadget.

Meanwhile, we meet the manufacturer anytime we pick up the manual to any gadget we purchase to read. To get ourselves acquainted with how to properly maximize a product and be freed from its misuse, the manual is a must-read. Funny enough, some gadgets are so small but with several pages of a manual on how to operate them. Life should be much better for many today if they took a break and meet the Manufacturer within the pages of His manual—the Bible.

I believe that knowing the mind of the Manufacturer would save us the misuse and misapplication of our lives to adventures and things that do not matter. This is why Dr. Myles Munroe said, *"When Purpose is not known, abuse is inevitable."*[7] You can imagine the number of prostitutes or anyone who sins towards their bodies we have in the world today. Sadly, these individuals have shunned the knowledge of the God that made them. The resultant effect of this ignorance is the misuse of their bodies and desire for their flesh more than God.

Even though these individuals misuse their bodies, the Manufacturer says in His manual, *"I want to bring you a future you hope for"* (Jeremiah 29:11). What a wonderful verse to stumble upon in God's manual for operating maximally the product that you are!

The manual also says, *"What? know ye not that your body is the temple of the Holy Ghost which is in you, which ye have of God, and ye are not your own? For ye are bought with a price: therefore, glorify God in your body, and in your spirit, which are God's."* 1 Corinthians 6:19-20 (KJV). If we must curb the increasing upsurge of the misuse of our lives, we must take our tangent from the manual that comes with the product—man.

Indeed, you need to thank God for purpose because He's the manufacturer. God is the first manufacturer, producer, creator, and inventor. The Bible reveals that God created heaven and earth and everything in them. (Genesis 1:1, 2:4) He's the mastermind behind nature and all creation. Everything that exists is a testament to His master craftsmanship. There's no manufacturer as creative, skillful, thoughtful, deliberate, resourceful and original as God.

Think about it. You can't find the materials He used to create the earth anywhere. What is sand made of? If you say small stones, then what are stones made of? What about the sun? If you explain that it's a ball of burning gases, how were the gases manufactured? How do they exist? Thinking about God's creative ability feels you with wonder. What is light made of? Too complex to wrap your mind around? Well, the point is, this manufacturer who's in a class of His own, created you.

Call to Action

How often do you communicate with your Manufacturer regarding the actualization of your purpose?

____

____

____

____

____

Prayer

Father, in the name of Jesus, I thank You for Your Word sent to me today. I pray that You will help me to stay align to my purpose on the earth. I will not be carried away and start to abuse the life You have given me. I have known You as my Manufacturer, I pray for the grace for connectivity to Your Spirit. In Jesus' name. Amen.

DAY 6
THE GIFT OF PURPOSE

Scriptural Text: "*John answered and said, A man can receive nothing, except it be given him from heaven.*"

–John 3:27 KJV

Inspiring Commentary

How do you feel whenever you are given a breath-taken gift? Grateful, loved, happy, or overwhelmed? Yes, gifts can call forth smiles and delight from our faces. But beyond the happiness and smiles gifts come with, our love, care, and connection with the Giver get re-affirmed or established. A valuable relationship will always result in constant and valuable giving. Wrapped in every act of giving is a communication of our love, commitment, and value.

In his book, 5 Love Languages: The Secret of Love That Last, Gary Chapman noted how important gifts are in the story of love between two couples. He tagged it a "visual symbol of love."[8] Here's the point. If men, who are evil, know how to give good gifts to one another, how much more God? Even though God gave His Son to us and later gave His Holy Spirit as a seal after salvation, purpose is another gift God has placed in every man to live an abundant life on the earth bringing glory to His name.

If a man's gift makes room for him and gives him access to great people, you'll remain limited until you know and receive the gift of purpose God has graciously placed within you. This is what changes everything. God took time to fashion you to meet a unique need on earth. When you find out what it is, you become a gift to your world. So, here's how it works: You discover God's gift of purpose for your life, walk in it and maximize it to the fullest, and you'll soon be received as a gift to your generation.

The truth is, when purpose is discovered, life becomes a treasured gift—every moment worth living. You begin to see yourself as priceless and worthy of the best things life offers. On the other hand, those who haven't discovered purpose don't cherish or treasure themselves.

A manufacturer's intent for designing or creating a product is its purpose. Purpose is the gift given by the manufacturer to the product. Why is it a gift? Because no product is useful without a purpose. Every product meets a need. Your cell phone meets a need; it has a purpose. Your dishwasher meets a need. Anything that isn't useful doesn't have purpose. So your purpose, which is bestowed on you by God, gives you value.

Consider how you purchase products you need around the house. First, you think of their usefulness. Whether it's groceries, kitchen utensils, gadgets or other household appliances, their purpose crosses your mind before you take out your wallet or purse. Therefore, purpose gives value and worth. It's a gift from the manufacturer. The absence of this gift produces worthlessness. Aren't you grateful for the gift of purpose?

Call to Action

The moment you discover your purpose, describe how it made you feel about yourself?

____

____

____

____

____

Prayer

Father, in the name of Jesus, I thank You for the gift of purpose. I know that my life will have been worthless without purpose. I know that I would have lacked direction without the gift of purpose. I thank You for giving order and beauty to my life through this powerful insight. For this, I am grateful. In Jesus' name. Amen.

DAY 7
USED ACCORDING TO PURPOSE

Scriptural Text: *"Let your light so shine before men, that they may see your good works, and glorify your Father which is in heaven."*

–Matthew 5:16 KJV

Inspiring Commentary

One of the doctor's responsibilities is to prescribe drugs for their patients to avoid misuse and damage to the body. According to an article written by Hannah Ritchie and Max Roser on Drug Use, *"Drug use is, directly and indirectly, responsible for 11.8 million death each year. Smoking, alcohol and drug use is an important risk factors for early death: 11.4 million die prematurely; as a result each year. And over 350,000 die from overdoses (alcohol and illicit drug use disorders) each year."*[9] As good as drugs may be in bringing health and vitality to lives, when misused can also lead to the early death of many!

Life is a trust that must be used according to purpose. Just like the body is deprived of health and soundness when drugs are misused, God's glory is veiled and at stake when men live outside purpose. God's glory is the end of the making of man. Hence, to live a life that doesn't maximally bring glory to God is living outside purpose! Let's take a glimpse at what the 24 elders do in the courts of heaven *"The four and twenty elders fall down before him that sat on the throne, and worship him that liveth for ever and ever, and cast their crowns before the throne, saying, "Thou art worthy, O Lord, to receive glory and honour and power: for thou hast created all things, and for Thy pleasure they are and were created."* " (Revelation 4:10-11 KJV)

There lies the zenith of our purpose—the glory of God. And, it happens to be that it is only when you use your life and giftings according to the purpose that glory goes back to God. Whatever isn't used as God intended is like disregarding God's decrees.

Dr Myles Munroe said, *"Purpose is when you know and understand what you were born to accomplish."*[10] Truly understanding purpose means getting the revelation of the driving force of purpose. Why does any manufacturer create a purpose? One word: desire. Now, for earthly manufacturers, they might be moved by the desires of others or their desire to meet the needs of their society. But in God's case, the driving force behind the purpose He gives to His creation is His desire.

What's the significance of being created in God's image and likeness? Well, first, you must understand that all products are designed according to their purpose. For instance, a sports car is designed for speed. Therefore, it's not built like a minivan. Its capacity for speed and its weight differs from a minivan's speed and weight. In the same way, man was designed according to His purpose. Although God created man to have dominion over all the works of His hands, man's dominion was designed to bring God glory. This should be your aim in all your endeavours.

Call to Action

What do you think is the outcome of living a life that doesn't bring glory to God?

____

____

____

____

____

Prayers

Father, in the name of Jesus, I thank You for the truth of Your Word today. I pray that my life will always bring glory to You. Deliver me from any selfish thought, intention and pursuit. Help me to always seek Your glory all the days of my life. As a light to the world, I shall shine, and all men shall see the great work You have done in my life. In Jesus' name. Amen.

DAY 8
GOD WAS INTENTIONAL

Scriptural Text: "*Then the LORD God formed the man of dust from the ground and breathed into his nostrils the breath of life, and the man became a living creature.*"

–Genesis 2:7 KJV

Inspiring Commentary

I found the first chapter of the book of Jeremiah intriguing. God said to Prophet Jeremiah, "*Before I formed thee in the belly I knew thee; and before thou camest forth out of the womb I sanctified thee, and I ordained thee a prophet unto the nations.*" (Jeremiah 1:5 NIV) I pray you hear God speak to you directly from this verse today. This verse of Scripture isn't only about Jeremiah—God was intentional about the birth of every human to this earth. He prescribed every single detail of your creation! Why? He fashioned you for a unique purpose.

Have you ever heard people say, "Oh, that was an unwanted pregnancy or child?" This is absurd for two reasons. First, does a child possess any power to be born? Second, was the child responsible for the sperm that fertilized the mother's egg? So, how in the world is a child supposed to carry the stigma of "an unwanted child" through their life? Even animals don't reproduce in the wild by mistake.

Amidst millions of sperms making their way to locate an egg, God chose you! I love the way Pastor Rick puts it "you are not an accident... Your birth was no mistake or mishap, and your life is no fluke of nature. Your parents may not have planned you, but God did. He was not at all surprised by your birth. In fact, He expected it."[11] Wow! What relief to know that God wanted you, and by His sovereign will, brought you to this earth. That is, your parents' consent or rejection notwithstanding. Before your parents could ever have you, God said *"...I knew you"* Not just that—I also separated you for a purpose.

Life isn't coincidental: it is intentional. Are you wondering if your life is intentional? The answer is yes. Why? Because someone had an intention for your existence. And just as God was intentional and meticulous about everything in nature, He was intentional when He created you. God didn't create sea creature until He had made their home—the sea.

Also, He created land before terrestrial creatures. Genesis chapter 1 reveals the order of creation, and no creature came too late or too early. God was intentional about every one of them. He exerted the same laser-like precision and meticulous intention in creating you. Why? Because He's the God of purpose.

Call to Action

What's your understanding of your intentionality with regards to your purpose on the earth?

____

____

____

____

____

Prayers

Father, in the name of Jesus, I thank You for been mindful of me. Thank You for been intentional about by creation and also my purpose. You didn't just speak me to existence, but You consciously molded me into Your image and after your likeness. I thank You for Your thoughtful precision and intentionality about me. I love You, Father. In Jesus' name. Amen.

DAY 9
BE FRUITFUL

Scriptural Text: *"So God created man in His own image, in the image of God, He created him; male and female, He created them. And God blessed them. And God said to them, "Be fruitful and multiply and fill the earth and subdue it, and have dominion over the fish of the sea and over the birds of the heavens and over every living thing that moves on the earth."*

–Genesis 1:27-28 KJV

Inspiring Commentary

A seed must first be subjected to death if it must bring forth abundance. It's planted for a season; the seed dies before it sprouts, flower and start to bear fruits. Jesus gave a secret to fruitfulness thus: *"I tell you the truth, unless a kernel of wheat is planted in the soil and dies, it remains alone. But its death will produce many new kernels—a plentiful harvest of new lives."* (John 12:24 NLT)

Seeds germinate in isolation; likewise, to grow and bring forth fruit in righteousness, there must be a time of separation from the place of confusion and noise. You must first be weaned from the bustling and busyness that deadens the consciousness of fruit-bearing unto God. The central goal of our purpose is to produce after our kind--God's life. Now, that's a profound statement to make. Fruitfulness goes beyond bearing physical seeds. It's spiritual!

When God said to them, "*...Be fruitful,*" we must be careful to know the kind of man God gave the mandate of fruitfulness unto. Even though the mandate to be fruitful could be captured both in the physical and spiritual planes, one would be right to say this is more spiritual than physical. I mean, of what use is it to produce and multiply godless seeds? The man God told to be fruitful was the man carrying God's life.

Much more than just being fruitful, you must be fruitful in Godliness. Many today are fruitful in darkness. And God desires that His children, carrying the incorruptible seed, reproduce their kinds everywhere. God wants to look down from heaven and find His kind scattered across the face of the earth. And how will this grand purpose be possible? Through the maximum use of God's gift of purpose.

In any field you find yourself in, God intends that many souls will be harvested unto Him by the mechanism of your purpose and gifts. This is the eternal counsel of God before making you. He intends that there's another man on the face of the earth through whom His kingdom would get populated. This is living a fruitful life. Through the fulfillment of your purpose, many are drawn into God's eternal kingdom.

Since you were made in God's image and likeness, your dominion on the earth should reveal and express God's nature and will. You were created to have God's desire in your heart and accomplish it. Your design—being like God—empowered you to accomplish this purpose. In line with purpose, you could be fruitful, multiply, fill the earth, subdue it and have dominion. Friend, your life is not solo, but you should multiply and replicate His life in you.

Call to Action

Have you discovered your purpose? In what way can you replicate your gifts and callings to the blessing of others?

Prayer

Father, in the name of Jesus, I thank You for the light from Your Word today. I pray for a deeper understanding of my purpose on the earth. I pray that You will help me to grow and multiply. Let me not be reduced in life, but I pray that You will stir up Your ability in me to multiply and bring glory to Your name. In Jesus' name. Amen.

DAY 10
HAVE DOMINION AND SUBDUE THE EARTH

Scriptural Text: *"And from Jesus Christ the faithful witness, the first-born of the dead, and the ruler of kings on earth. To Him who loves us and has freed us from our sins by His blood, and made us a kingdom, priests to His God and Father, to Him be glory and dominion forever and ever. Amen."*

–Revelations 1:5-6 KJV

Inspiring Commentary

Amidst all that God created at the beginning of time, only man was made in His image and likeness. And that was significant for the role He wanted them to play in creation. Man is the head of God's creation, charged with the responsibility to put everything in order. As a result, God bequeathed to man authority to rule and dominate the earth. Hence, God ruled the earth through man. The habitat for man's dominion is earth--nothing in it can tame man.

According to Darwin's law of natural selection, the phrase "surviv-al of the fittest" became popularized. What does this mean? In 1859 Charles Darwin wrote a book about the evolution theory where he submitted "*It's not the strongest that survives the jungle, nor the most intelligent. But the one most responsive to change!*"[12] The lions in the wild are most associated with this concept. Why?

Despite the size or frame of lions, they are commonly thought to be the strongest animals in the jungle and the fiercest predator. The lion takes dominion of the wide not because he's the biggest or smartest animal but due to their tenacity and courage in securing their domains and displaying stability in the face of any other animal.

The lion lives with a majestic consciousness of their innate abilities and strength to rule the jungle. To this end, King Solomon lamented thus: "*I have seen servants upon horses, and princes walking as servants upon the earth.*" (Ecclesiastes 10:7 NIV) Even though the believer has been given so much power and authority to rule and have dominion upon the earth, we see many still walking on foot like servants today. Even though the earth is the Lord's and the fullness thereof, doesn't it seem the devil is the real owner of the earth?

Well, this is for a simple reason. Man, that is supposed to be God's agent of extending His dominion upon the earth, now lives an ordinary life. Meanwhile, every child of God is supernatural in make-up. Jesus' life is proof of what it means to have dominion. He defied sickness, raised the dead, walked on water, cursed a tree to its root, turned water into wine, and did several impossible things. He was absolutely in charge through the power of the age to come working effortlessly in Him.

Like Adam, you were designed to reveal God's glory through your nature and character and influence your environment. In the general mandate to have dominion resides your individual mandate. There's a particular kind of influence and fruitfulness God wants you to have in a given field; you are not just there to struggle for promotions but to replicate the life of Christ in that area.

Call to Action

How well have you taken over in the area of your purpose? What are the challenges that are keeping you from advancing further?

____

____

____

____

____

Prayer

Father, in the name of Jesus, I thank You for creating me with the ability to dominate and subdue the earth. I pray for the insight to see myself as You have created me. I pray for the resilience to overcome every challenge in life so that I may remain in dominion in every field of endeavour that You have put me. In Jesus' name. Amen.

DAY 11
VESSELS WANTED

Scriptural Text: *"The heaven, even the heavens, are the LORD'S: but the earth hath he given to the children of men."*

–Psalms 115:16 KJV

Inspiring Commentary

What comes to mind immediately when you read today's text? Isn't it apparent what God willed to man in that verse? Before we look deeper into why God willed the earth to man, let's see the make-up of man.

Man is a tripartite being, that is, body, soul, and spirit. 1 Thessalonians 5:23 (NIV) captures this vividly, *"And the God of peace Himself sanctify you wholly, and may your spirit and soul and body be preserved complete, without blame, at the coming of our Lord Jesus Christ"* So, according to this Scripture, those three parts are crucial elements that God's sanctifying power must reach to make it wholesome.

Now, our soul is our personality, who we are. And we think, reason, remember and wonder through this handle. All our experience of emotions like happiness, love, sorrow, anger, relief, and compassion flows from the soul. If this part of man isn't there, to resolve, choose, and make decisions becomes impossible.

And the human spirit is the deepest part of our being. The aspect of you that got quickened backed to life at salvation. Using this innermost part, we can contact God in the spiritual realm. It's worthy of note, however, that no other creature was created by God with this essential component—the spirit. And finally, our body exists on the outward, the material, and contacts the tangible things of the world using our five physical senses.

This is where the uniqueness of this creature called man is. With his spirit, he can touch and relate with God's realm; with the body, he can relate with the realm of the physical. With this makeup, both God and the devil know man is a viable means to reach the earth. God does not want zombies for children. By the instrumentality of your will, you must choose God and agree that He flows ceaselessly through you. So that by a yielded living, God's presence becomes tangible upon the earth. Man is a vessel God intends to flow through. Hence, the reason for the essential parts of man's make-up.

God in His infinite wisdom has chosen to fulfill His purposes for the earth through human vessels. This means God won't act unless it's through people who have yielded themselves to Him. Why? Isn't God Almighty? Why can't He just ignore man and do what He wants. It's because of Genesis 1:26-28. When God gave man dominion over the earth, it also made it illegal for spirits without human bodies to be the major actors on the earth. God made the earth man's domain, making him the primary actor on earth. Every transaction spirits want to carry out must be through human vessels. Therefore, God looks for vessels to fulfill His purposes.

However, God doesn't look for human vessels in the sense that He scouts around for who He can give a purpose. No. God gives a purpose to every person He creates. His search for vessels is an invitation for people to accept His will for them and yield to instruments of His divine purpose. God desires to fill the earth with His glory. The dominion mandate is still ongoing. Every human being has a distinct part to play. There are many purposes embedded in one general purpose. But God is still seeking for yielded vessels. Why yielded vessels? Because although every human being is factory fitted for purpose by design, we need to be molded in God's hands until we become the kind of vessel He's pleased with. Are you ready to be yielded to God's will?

Call to Action

Have you responded to God call on your life? Are you a worthy vessel for the Master to use for His purpose on the earth?

____

____

____

____

____

Prayer

Father, in the name of Jesus, I thank You for creating me as a vessel that You can fill. I pray that You occupy me afresh today and make me worthy to express Your glory. I pray that my will embody Your purpose for mankind and the world around me. I pray that heaven will not be in need of man when I'm alive. I pray that You align me as a vessel unto honor for Your glory. In Jesus' name. Amen.

DAY 12
A CONDUIT

Scriptural Text: *"And I sought for a man among them who should build up the wall and stand in the breach before me for the land, that I should not destroy it, but I found none."*

–Ezekiel 22:30 ESV

Inspiring Commentary

According to the Merriam-Webster dictionary, a conduit is *"a natural or artificial channel through which something (such as a fluid) is conveyed. It's also a pipe, tube, or tile for protecting electric wires or cables."*[13] In simple terms, a conduit is a thing fashioned to channel or give access to something liquid or fluid. A pipe, for instance, gives access to water from one source to another. It aids transport and transmission.

God has fashioned man to function by default the same way a pipe conveys water from a reservoir into containers. When a man understands and walks in his purpose, God sees a door to move on the earth. God's entire resources can then flow through that man to anywhere God desires for them to go. If God wants to heal, He wants conduits through whom He can dispense His healing virtues and power.

Man is a legal occupant on earth and what happens upon it largely depends on him. This is why a heart God hasn't conquered will give a place to the devil to flow his demonic intelligence through. So, the devil seeks to pervade our space by sin and make us enemies of God. That way, he can further establish his rule on earth. When the devil rules your heart, he also control over your space. Hence, because your purpose is your license upon and to the earth, the devil will like to give you a new pursuit alien to the eternal purpose of God for your life. This is to the intent that He may flow His counsel through you.

Friend, how do you know you're here to do something special and unique? By understanding that purpose is a conduit into the earth. Remember how we said that nothing exists without a purpose? That every manufacturer has an intent for their product? Well, your purpose is why you are existing. There's no illegal human being. Everyone comes with God's seal of approval because we're packaged to fulfill purpose.

Jeremiah 1:5 (KJV) says, *"Before I formed thee in the belly I knew thee; and before thou camest forth out of the womb I sanctified thee, and I ordained thee a prophet unto the nations."* These are God's words to Prophet Jeremiah. Here, God reveals that before Jeremiah existed, God knew him—had the idea of him from start to finish. The word sanctified in the above verse means to separate or consecrate for special use. So Jeremiah was prepared by God as a unique instrument in His hands. Finally, God ordained him to be a prophet unto the nations, allotting him purpose. All these things happened before Jeremiah came into the earth. So, make up your mind that you will be that conduit through which God's manifest presence and power are manifested on the earth.

Call to Action

What has God separated you for among others? What instruction have you received from God regarding your assignment and calling?

____

____

____

____

____

Prayer

Father, in the name of Jesus, thank You for making me understand the true essence of my being. I pray that by the help of the Holy Spirit, You will make a worthy conduit of Your power and glory. Your Word shows that You are always in search of man that will partner with You to bring to pass Your purpose on the earth, Lord, I submit myself as a worthy conductor of Your power and grace for my generation. In Jesus' name. Amen.

DAY 13

LOOK UNTO GOD!

Scriptural Text: *"for we walk by faith, not by sight"*

–2 Corinthians 5:7 ESV

Inspiring Commentary

In the book of Numbers 13, Moses had sent 12 spies to the land of Canaan to know the state of the land. Only two—Joshua and Caleb- out of twelve—brought good and faith-propelled feedback. What they saw was shaped by their knowledge and understanding of God. So, while the others saw defeat and fear built up in their hearts, Caleb saw differently *"…Caleb stilled the people before Moses, and said, "Let us go up at once, and possess it; for we are well able to overcome it." "* (Numbers 13:30 KJV)

The response of the men that went with Caleb and Joshua was typical of men who walk by sight. They judge by the hearing of the ears, and little challenges turn them into fraidy cats. See what these men said; *"But the men that went up with him said, we be not able to go up against the people; for they are stronger than we." And they brought up an evil report of the land which they had searched unto the children of Israel, saying, The land, through which we have gone to search it, is a land that eateth up the inhabitants thereof; and all the people that we saw in it are men of a great stature. And there we saw the giants, the sons of Anak, which come of the giants: and we were in our own sight as grasshoppers, and so we were in their sight."* (Numbers 13:31-33 KJV)

Too often, when we look into our situation and shortcomings, fear and resentment follow. At such an instance, the best place to turn to fulfill God's eternal purpose for your life isn't the giants around you or your weaknesses, but God. When we see ourselves as what others say about us, we become weak in actualizing our destiny. But when we look unto God despite our weaknesses, streams of divine strength begin to flow into and from us.

The truth is, some people are looking at others for validation, direction and meaning. Others are looking within themselves. But to understand where purpose is found, answer this question. Where does a product get its purpose from? Where do consumers of that product get the purpose of that product? Obviously, it's from the manufacturer. Only the person who made the product can truly define its use. In fact, only the manufacturer or creator of a product can maximize its full potential.

So since your purpose originates from God, it can only be found in Him. Don't waste your time trying to figure out when you can go to God. It's like ignoring a product's manual and trying to be creative. You'll damage the product. Likewise, not going to God, your manufacturer to receive the revelation of purpose will affect you negatively. You'll waste time on things you weren't created for.

Here's a shortcut: go to God to discover purpose. Some people are used to dreaming without God. They think they have big dreams. But who can out dream God? Your unique purpose is with God. It was first His desire before it became your dream. So, ask Him in prayers today and open your heart to receive answers.

Call to Action

What have people said to you in the past that you believed about yourself?

____

____

____

____

____

Have you conquered the negative voices, or you are still living a lie?

____

____

____

____

____

Prayer

Father, in the name of Jesus, I thank You for the insight from Your Word. I know many sounds and voices around; I pray that You help me shut out any other voice that is not from You. Open my ears to hear what You are saying concerning me and also see what You are showing me. I will not be lost in the crowd, but You will help me to stand out, seeking and pursuing my unique purpose in life. In Jesus' name. Amen.

DAY 14
MADE BY FOLLOWING

Scriptural Text: "*And He said to them, 'Follow Me, and I will make you fishers of men.'*"

–Matthew 4:19 ESV

Inspiring Commentary

Mentoring is one of the prime ingredients to success in any sphere. No one is an island of knowledge. And where you're heading, many have been there. So, you need those who have gone ahead of you to help you place your foot in the right spot as you grow in your assignment, purpose, or calling. One of the beauties of mentoring is that it saves you lots of heartache.

Have you ever thought of why most people end up becoming nothing even though full of desires and gifts? Hey, the answer is simple! No adequate guardian and culturing. Truth is, we become what/who we follow. Every athlete values the impact of their coach. A student has no future without a competent teacher. And an apprentice will learn nothing except under a skilled master.

That's just how life is fashioned. There is no other way to maximize your potential than to submit to be an ardent follower of the God of all purposes. It's so fascinating that many want to know the mind of

God but are far from Him. Followership gives birth to transformation and growth. It can open doors, inspire, support, and encourage people to realize their potential and achieve them.

Peter never knew what He could do until Jesus took him through the school of discipleship for three and a half years. After his classes under the Master, he received the seal of the Holy Spirit, and the timid, fearful, and unstable Peter became a strong figure in executing God's purpose.

Much will be kept unused and unchallenged into reality in your life without getting committed to following the Giver of life and purpose. There can be no Joshua without the grooming of Moses, no Elisha without submitting to Elijah's instructions, and there will be no mighty army of David without years of Adullam training. Till today men are still made by following.

Before any product goes to the market and is made available to the public, it spends quality time with the manufacturer. It isn't shown off to the public until the manufacturer's ownership and craft are visible in its design.

There are famous artists whose works are known by the stroke of their brushes and their distinctive genius. Every great master-creator leaves their fingerprint on their creation. It's difficult not to acknowledge their masterful work. God does the same thing with His choice vessels. Thus intimacy with God is the kind produced by the making process. As you get to know God, you get to know yourself more and discover your purpose on the earth.

An excellent example of this branding work of the manufacturer on His products can be seen in the life of Jesus' disciples. Although Jesus had ascended into heaven, His work was evident in their lives. People saw them and could trace their conduct and passion back to Jesus. So, keep following and allow God to make you into what you were designed to be.

Call to Action

Are you a follower of the Father? What practical ways can we follow Jesus until we are made?

____

____

____

____

____

Prayer

Father, in the name of Jesus, I see the validity of following hard after You for my making. I pray that You help me to keep following hard after You. By the help of the Holy Spirit, give me a heart that trusts and seeks to follow You to the end until I become all You have made me. I pray that I will never draw back from following You. In Jesus' name. Amen.

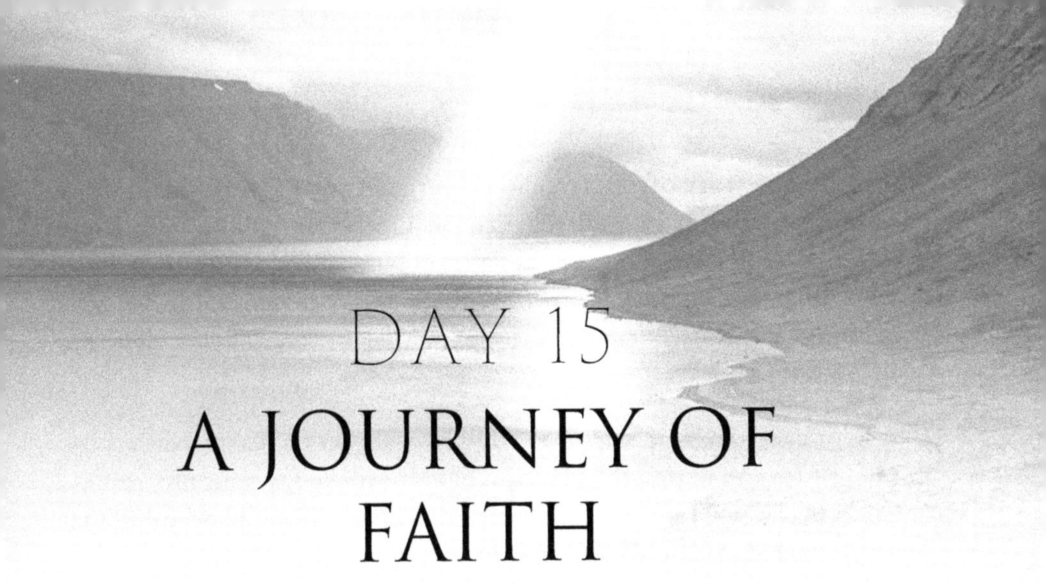

DAY 15

A JOURNEY OF FAITH

Scriptural Text: *"but the righteous shall live by his faith."*

–Habakkuk 2:4 KJV

Inspiring Commentary

With the ever thriving motivational tips and tricks we have all over the place, it's easy to run your destiny on autopilot and push God to the background. Once, you only go when you couldn't figure out your way anymore. You can be skillful in planning, erudite in knowing all the principles, and yet mess up the purposes of God for your life by falling into a self-help and self-effort mindset.

I know quite well that mastery comes through repetition. But hey! One thing is key here for me to tell you today, nobody walks in the fullness of God's purpose being the pilot of their life's affair. No matter how intelligent you are, you aren't all-knowing or omnipotent. This is why our plans may fail, our projections may be wrong, and speculation often may be incorrect. So, you need to be in relationship with the all-seeing God to walk through the earth fulfilled.

David Burns once wrote, *"Faith is: dead to doubts, dumb to discouragements, blind to impossibilities."*[14] To walk in purpose, faith is key! We do not just need faith to fulfill destiny; it's the currency on which life thrives. The story of the Israelites is a rich locus for how the journey of faith works. It is total reliance on God's infallibility. The Bible described and sectioned the children of Israel into two groups: those who obtained the promise through faith and patience and those who perished in the wilderness through unbelief. They never saw the Promised Land.

Not everyone with a glorious destiny walks in its reality. Faith is the catalyst for the impossible. If God has a purpose for your life, rest assured that it will only take His strength to pull through and fulfill that purpose. Hence, we do not just need God to discover purpose, it is only through Him that we thrive in it.

In Genesis 12:1 (NLT), the Bible says, *"The LORD had said to Abram, "Leave your native country, your relatives, and your father's family, and go to the land that I will show you."* Remember that in Joshua 24:2-3, the Bible reveals that Abraham was an idol worshiper like his father and brother.

So God's command to leave his country, his kindred, and his father's house was a revolutionary change for Abraham. He was turning his back on the familiar and moving towards the unknown. He was rejecting those dumb idols and choosing the living God. Abraham had come to crossroads where he needed to make a life-altering decision.

In truth, everyone that will know God deeply must arrive at this valley of decision. You must choose Him above all else. God commanded Abraham to leave all that he knew to follow Him. The nature of His call gives us a glimpse into how those who will discover purpose must live—by faith. You may have seen the picture of your purpose, but you need to journey with God by faith to arrive there.

Call to action

Think of an experience when you were faced with a challenge on your journey and how you overcame it with God's help.

____

____

____

____

____

Prayer

Father, in the name of Jesus, I thank You for the insight about faith. I know the journey to fulfilling my purpose is not a sprint; there will be curves and bends; I pray that You help me master the act of following You by faith. Let me not be full of myself, but I pray for the faith to follow You till the end. No matter the doubts, strengthen my faith in You at all times so I can arrive in spite of challenges. In Jesus' name. Amen.

DAY 16
TRIGGERS OF PURPOSE

Scriptural Text: *"Wherefore I put thee in remembrance that thou stir up the gift of God, which is in thee by the putting on of my hands."*

–2 Timothy 1:6 KJV

Inspiring Commentary

Throughout human history, several weapons have been used in warfare, hunting, self-defense, law enforcement, and for criminal purposes. One prominent weapon of war today is the rifle. Despite all the weapons used in history, rifles have come to dominate the battlefield ever since their debut. Out of all the important parts of a rifle, the trigger plays a unique role in execution.

A trigger is said to be "a part of a gun that causes the gun to fire when pressed."[15] The word may also be defined as "a small device that releases a spring or catch and so sets off a mechanism."[16] In other words, the trigger is the initiator or that which sponsors the operation of a thing--that which makes functional.

For instance, a rifle could be despised as long as the trigger isn't pulled. An electric plant or generator may never fulfill its purpose in an office until it is triggered. In the same way you could assume no bullet is inside a rifle until the trigger is pulled, you will never experience the effect of your purpose until you understand purpose triggers. Purpose triggers make obvious in you what you never thought was there! Let's make a list of some.

The first trigger: "whatever makes you angry and uncomfortable" is a pointer and a trigger of what you're made to focus your energy to fix. Elders were in the temple in the time of Jesus buying and selling until He came in there to chase them out! He was driven by purpose. This isn't anger that flows out of hate but love for God!

The second trigger: "Unflinching passion for a course" is proof that God has kept something on your inside to get a job done, the enemy notwithstanding. Remember Nehemiah? Several darts of discouragement came at him but he kept building the walls of Jerusalem.

The third trigger: "Some of your giftings are pointers to your purpose." You must realize that not everybody does what you do with ease. By makeup, there are gifts God has kept in you as triggers of your purpose and assignment. Find them!

Reading through the Bible, you'll discover that it's God's will that His people begin to prepare for purpose right from birth. Many parents don't know this but purpose is first the responsibility of the parent. Godly parents make purpose discovery and fulfillment easier for their children. They get the revelation from God and pass it on to their children. We see this severally in the Bible where God reveals the purpose of a child to the parents.

Proverbs 22:6 (KJV) says, *"Train up a child in the way he should go: and when he is old, he will not depart from it."* The home is supposed to be a training center. Parents are the trainers and children, the trainees.

Now, you might feel you know this Scripture. Yes, it means to raise children with Godly values and they'll live by those values forever. But there's another meaning. It means that parents are to find out where their children are going. Yes! So you need to ask, "What's his or her purpose?" "What is he or she created to achieve?" Sometimes, from just paying attention to your child's creative tendencies, passion and talent, you can get a glimpse of their purpose."

Call to Action

What are some of the triggers you have discovered that are pointers to your purpose in life?

____

____

____

____

____

Prayers

Father, in the name of Jesus, I thank You for the passion and gift You have put in me. I pray that You open my eyes and strengthen me to stir this gift up accordingly. I ask that the triggers in me will remain active and the fire will keep burning. Just as You helped Nehemiah to overcome every darts of discouragement thrown at him, help me to also stand strong on the path of my purpose. In Jesus' name. Amen.

DAY 17
CONSECRATED

Scriptural Text: *"Now in a wealthy home there are not only gold and silver vessels, but also ones made of wood and of clay, and some are for honorable use, but others for ignoble use. So if someone cleanses himself of such behavior, he will be a vessel for honorable use, set apart, useful for the Master, prepared for every good work."*

–2 Timothy 2:20-21 KJV

Inspiring Commentary

The word consecration comes from the Greek word "*hagiazo,*" which means "to render or acknowledge, or to be venerable or hallow. To separate from what is profane and dedicate to God. It could also mean to purify."[17] When a thing is consecrated, its purpose is clearly defined, and it is used for that singular course. Hence, if a man gets dedicated or set apart unto God, he starts living for God alone!

It's sad to see how many believers do not understand what it means to be sold out to God anymore today. They want to have God on their side and still be in the good books of ungodly men. It doesn't work that way! The life God will use for His holy purposes; He doesn't share with things that corrupt. A heart that will house God must be fortified with the love of God.

From today's text, we see that there is a purging that results in a noble use by God. Before God uses a person, He takes them through the practice of consecration, and they maintain that posture for the rest of their lives. This principle must guide you as you walk with God. He always sets apart those He chooses as His vessel.

So at divinely appointed intervals, God will give you instructions that will lead to consecration. This means that if God would use you to fulfill purpose, you must be consecrated. And if you will yield to consecration, you must understand and love obedience.

Understand that your consecration will not happen by accident. Neither will it occur without your participation. God's role is to give instructions concerning your separation; yours is to obey Him. Your level of obedience determines whether or not you fulfill purpose. And if you delay in obedience, it will also affect your season of manifestation. So, it's time to clean up so you can hook up with God's assignment for your life.

Call to Action

What areas of your life do you need the consecration of the Holy Spirit.

____

____

____

____

____

It's time to take a conscious step and pray about it.

____

____

____

____

____

Prayer

Father, in the name of Jesus, I thank You for this unique call to consecration. I pray that You purify me from the inside out. Clean me through and through until my heart becomes a home for You. I understand that I can't walk with You to fulfill my purpose without being cleaned up. I pray You to sanctify me by Your blood and make me fit for Your purpose. In Jesus' name. Amen.

DAY 18

HIDDEN WISDOM

Scriptural Text: *"It is the glory of God to conceal a thing; but the honour of kings is to search out a matter."*

–Proverbs 25:2 KJV

Inspiring Commentary:

The purpose of the believer is directly linked to God. Hence, it must be diligently sought out. God hides nothing from His children but hides for them. This is to say that the process of seeking to discover purpose is bait to know God more. The more the knowledge of God gets unveiled to you, the more the blueprint of your life gets handed out to you.

Oh, you feel a sense of satisfaction when you search out a matter. It brings honour! While on that search, you wouldn't have only discovered purpose but meet with the God of purpose. Purpose is revealed, not stumbled upon. Gold is one of the most valuable items in the world, isn't it? Yet it is not found somewhere on the surface. Think about it for a moment; how deep do you think you'll have to dig to find gold?

For instance, the Oregon Gold deposit, "one of the two types of deposit that require digging, can be found at an approximate depth of between 4000 feet and 15,000 feet. While Epithermal Gold deposit can be found at approximately 5,000 feet."[18] Funny enough, many resources must be invested in pursuing mining gold. It comes out in raw form, and after other processing procedures, it becomes honourable to all. Likewise, your purpose isn't commonplace.

Your purpose is a mystery, and it has to be revealed, not created or conjured through ambition. Every person who desires to fulfill their purpose must have a revelation divinely granted by God. Now, the fact that your purpose is a mystery, a pearl of hidden wisdom, doesn't make it difficult to access. If God concealed it from human eyes, why search it out, right? Why believe He would even want to unveil it? Why hide it in the first place? Yes, the nature of purpose as a mystery causes a little frustration. But that's for those who don't understand why it was hidden.

The first thing you should know is that your purpose is a kingdom mystery. If you know what Jesus said about kingdom mysteries, you should be rejoicing already. Purpose is a kingdom mandate. It is for the kingdom and of the kingdom. Earlier, we saw that God has a desire. He wants His glory to overshadow the earth and be made manifest to every creature. Well, God's glory can only be revealed through the expansion of His kingdom because it is the domain of His authority.

So, draw closer to God, and as His light shines on you, every scale and darkness falls off your heart, and you begin to discover what you were made for.

Call to Action

What step are you taking to unravel the hidden wisdom of God regarding your purpose?

____

____

____

____

____

Prayers

Father, in the name of Jesus, I understand that You are all-knowing, and nothing is hidden from You. You know all things, and You only reveal what we need to know per time. Therefore, I pray today that You reveal my purpose to me. Let me not live in oblivion to the fullness of what You have called me to be. Give me the wisdom to know where You have assigned me on the earth to manifest. In Jesus' name. Amen.

DAY 19
TRUST AND PURPOSE

Scriptural text: *"And we know that in all things God works for the good of those who love Him, who have been called according to His purpose,"*

–Romans 8:28-29 NIV

Inspiring Commentary

Trust isn't demanded, given, or coveted. It is earned by consistent proof of loyalty and commitment to a course or someone. We live and make decisions each moment on our level of trust. How do you know if you take a bottle of Coke, it isn't going to get you sick? Why would you trust your life into a pilot's hand even though the aircraft could crash in the air? Trust is simply to choose to be vulnerable and committed in the face of possible challenges. We trust despite fear and uncertainty.

Abraham had waited for several years for Isaac to be born when God said to him, "Some time later God tested Abraham; He called to him, "Abraham!" And Abraham answered, "Yes, here I am!" "Take your son," God said, "your only son, Isaac, whom you love so much, and go to the land of Moriah. There on a mountain that I will show you, offer him as a sacrifice to me." (Genesis 22:1-2 GNB) What would you have done? Obviously, Abraham had no clue why God demanded for his only child, but he trusted Him all the same.

Why? He had faith in God's ability to kill and make alive. Abraham seems to have a clear understanding of God's love, integrity, and altruism. He knew God can not do evil. That perceived sense of God's benevolence made him set out the next morning on that journey of obedience. To fulfill destiny and purpose, trust is vital. If you do not believe God can help you, you'll refuse Him through unbelief when He demands your obedience. And God doesn't measure how much we are committed to Him by what we say but how promptly we obey Him.

You must be ready to trust God despite uncertainties. For faithful is God who chose you from the foundation of the world; He's able to keep His promises. That is, even when it doesn't look like it—He's still working all things together for good!

1 Corinthians 2:9 (AMP) says, "But, on the contrary, as the Scripture says, *"What eye has not seen and ear has not heard and has not entered into the heart of man, [all that] God has prepared (made and keeps ready) for those who love Him [who hold Him in affectionate reverence, promptly obeying Him and gratefully recognizing the benefits He has bestowed]."*

One recurrent theme in both Scriptures above is that they describe people of purpose as lovers of God. This is because purpose demands sacrifice, consecration and death to personal ambition. Those who take up the cross of purpose have left all to follow Jesus, and He can trust them with His purposes. So I call you today to a love walk with God and throw all at His feet in absolute surrender and trust. He has a calling for you, and rest assured that He will help you fulfill it.

Call to Action

What do you think are some factors or events that make people trust God less regarding the fulfillment of their purpose?

____

____

____

____

____

Prayers

Father, in the name of Jesus, I thank You for the fresh dose of trust I received today from Your Word. I pray that You help me to stay true to You. Like Abraham, I pray that You help me trust You always as I walk daily towards my purpose. Today, I receive a new heart wrapped in absolute faith in You to see me through to the end. In Jesus' name. Amen.

DAY 20
MERCY DROPS

Scriptural Text: "*…For He makes His sun to shine on bad and good people alike, and gives rain to those who do good and to those who do evil.*"
–Matthew 5:45 GNB

Inspiring Commentary

Have you ever wondered at God's heart of love and mercy even to the unworthy? Think about some of the renowned vile leaders the world has ever witnessed. All of them were intelligent, gifted, and highly diplomatic. Which of them would you have allowed to stay alive, sparing them a single day if you were in God's shoes? Think about former German dictator of Germany—Adolf Hitler, Saddam Hussein—the Iraq dictator, or Joseph Stalin—the dictator of the Soviet Union. They all wrote their names on the sands of time with the blood of the innocent.

Yet, they lived on God's free grace and shared provisions. The Bible reveals in the above text, "*…For He makes His sun to shine on bad and good people alike, and gives rain to those who do good and to those who do evil.*" (Matthew 5:45 GNB) What many outside God's counsel calls purpose today are just drops of God's mercy, not the pure showers of blessings over their lives.

Yes, some might even argue that it's possible to stumble into one's purpose without an intimate relationship with God. That sounds like a valid point of argument until we probe what the world defines as purpose. I am not talking about a self-endued or American-Dream-influenced sought-of thing. I'm talking about a divine purpose. A sign of a restaurant isn't the restaurant.

God may give you mercy drops—signs and signals of your purpose—to pull you to Himself. But the real secrets are revealed when you get to Him. Only a "Damascus encounter" with the self-willed and ambitious Paul can open the heavens for a shower of blessings.

Here's an amazing illustration: Moses and the burning bush. *"Now Moses kept the flock of Jethro his father in law, the priest of Midian: and he led the flock to the backside of the desert, and came to the mountain of God, even to Horeb. And the angel of the LORD appeared unto him in a flame of fire out of the midst of a bush: and he looked, and, behold, the bush burned with fire, and the bush was not consumed. And Moses said, I will now turn aside, and see this great sight, why the bush is not burnt. And when the LORD saw that he turned aside to see, God called unto him out of the midst of the bush, and said, Moses, Moses. And he said, Here am I. And he said, Draw not nigh hither: put off thy shoes from off thy feet, for the place whereon thou standest is holy ground."* (Exodus 3:1-5 KJV)

There are some lessons to learn in this passage regarding mercy drops. Check it out:

1. God draws us to Himself through supernatural means. It might not always be spectacular, but it's always supernatural. God drew Moses to Himself by creating a supernatural attraction: *the bush that burned with fire, and was not consumed.* At this point, Moses wasn't intimate with God. Hence, the need for God to draw him. Some people mistake God's act of attracting them to Himself as the unveiling of the entirety of God's plan. No, He only draws us so we can decide to pay attention to Him. This is a mercy drop, a working of God's grace.

2. God expects us to make a life-changing decision. *Moses said, I will now turn aside, and see this great sight, why the bush is not burnt.* He decided to pay attention to what God was showing him. He

> received the trickle of revelation occasioned by God's mercy and decided to maximize it. His heart was engaged. When God draws, He calls us and expects a response. It's tragic to stop at the drawing or attraction stage.

Why not embrace His mercy today and turn from the wrong pursuit into a life of fulfillment with the God of purpose.

Call to Action

What area of your life do you earnestly desire God's mercy? List it out and pray about it today.

____

____

____

____

____

Prayers

Father, in the name of Jesus, I thank You primarily for Your mercy. I am absolutely nothing without Your mercy. My breath, by standing, my health, my family, and all that I am today are by Your mercy. And so, I ask today for Your mercy, not just drops of it but the rain of Your mercy. I pray that You will position and reposition me on the path of Your purpose for my life by Your mercy. In Jesus' name. Amen.

DAY 21
WALKING IN GOD'S WILL

Scriptural Text: *"Then said I, Lo, I come (in the volume of the book it is written of me,) to do thy will, O God."*

–Hebrews 10:7 KJV

Inspiring Commentary

We live daily, making choices from many options. But at some point in our lives, we are faced with major and defining decisions while we wonder what best option would fit. Who should I marry? What course do I study? Should I adopt a child? What about taking a job offer that may hamper your relationship with God? Here is where the problem is—who should win and influence my final answers and choices in life? My transient self-will or God's eternal counsel.

How many in our world today tend to worship a *zombie God*. One that never leads the person to their ultimate purpose in life. One that never desires to live life more abundantly if they would only yield to His will. But many are used to praying to Him with commands, demanding their way. That's the portrait countless people have of God today. So, they make grand plans and just ask God to put His stamp of agreement on it. God doesn't set the tone of their lives. But the true

God of the Bible is controlled and guided by His will, not our godless appetites.

God isn't committed to finishing what He hasn't started. If He must be the Omega, He must first be the Alpha. Hence, a man who hasn't crossed the rope of selfishness and ambition can never serve God's will. The end of all he does will be himself—not God. He can give anything as long as God promises to pay him back multiple folds. He serves for what he can get in return. But a man that has lost his will for good in God, soars effortlessly to the peak of his purpose.

A surrendered man doesn't struggle with God's instructions, he simply obeys them. In fact, God's heartbeat becomes his, and joy fills his heart anytime he does God's will. That's the kind of specie that can walk in divine purpose. On the other hand, a shipwreck is inevitable when men are bent on their ways. Truthfully, pursuing personal ambition reduces your usefulness in God's universal plan. God says, "I have a purpose for you." But full of pride, you answer and walk away, "I have better plans for myself." Really? That's a height of ignorance of who God is. Whatever God gives is really the best! You can't get it any better anywhere.

Moses wasn't a rebel. He just made disqualifying mistakes. He failed to see that God's will is to be accomplished how He sees fit. You can't do whatever you like with the will of God. Now, God deals so severely with someone who is committed to Him but failed to take himself out of the equation. What about someone who struggles with the will of God?

You may wonder, "Can a person struggle with the will of the Almighty God?" Yes, many times, we do; it's a human trait. We often want our way. No wonder what passes for dreams and purposes in our day is a person's ability to picture the kind of life they desire and make plans to achieve it. This kind of thinking and attitude ignores God.

Proverbs 19:21 (NLT) says, *"You can make many plans, but the LORD's purpose will prevail."* So articulate and profound, right? God's purpose will always override your plans. When something prevails, it proves to be more powerful or superior. This shows that if you still have a will apart from God's will, it will always stand in the way. So, let it go and let God have His way in your life.

Call to Action

What are your plans and desire that you know are conflicting with God's will for your life? It's time to hang them up and follow through with God's will.

____

____

____

____

____

Prayer

Father, in the name of Jesus, I come humbly before You today to ask for the grace to walk in Your will. Deliver me from being self-willed and articulate on my way, help me to let go of my plans and always seek to do only Your will. I know that my purpose is wrapped in Your will for my life; let Your will be my biggest desire. In Jesus' name. Amen.

DAY 22
STICK WITH GOD'S PLAN!

Scriptural Text: *"And when they had brought their ships to land, they forsook all, and followed Him"*

–Luke 5:11 KJV

Inspiring Commentary

God created man with creative abilities. And this, more often than not, makes us ignorantly think we are self-sufficient and masters in our little empire called earth. Many are even trying to think God out of their head right now. We are good at devising several counsels alien to God and His will. Yes, we've made several inventions and discoveries, but that never makes us all-knowing and all-powerful.

Hence, if you must walk in purpose and fulfill divine ordination, you must be subject to God's leading at every step of the way. On the path of purpose fulfillment, creativity is highly restricted by God's leading and instructions. So that if God hasn't commanded it, you have no business doing it! You can't be more intelligent than the One who enabled your thinking faculty and sustains its functionality. To have the blueprint of your destiny available, you must maintain a search into the depths of God's heart.

God commanded Noah to build an ark of preservation for his generation with a well-detailed plan. God gave the call and assignment; therefore, He must also give the plan for what He wanted. You have no liberty to build anything or do anything that God never commanded. All that Jesus did was captured on the pages of the Jewish Torah—the Old Testament. He simply followed the written plan for His life till the point of death. He never altered any part, leaving us an example that we should follow.

Therefore, you must know God's plan and stick with it to fulfill your destiny and purpose! There is no room for unhealthy comparison and strife in pursuing your purpose and destiny. You look and compare yourself with only One—Jesus Christ. Why? He is the Author and the Finisher of your faith and election!

The purging results from taking a detour or doing something totally outside God's plan. God doesn't just have a purpose for you; He has a strategy concerning how it will be fulfilled. When you replace God's strategy with yours, you will make costly mistakes. Now, to restore you to the path of purpose, God has to purge you. This process is painful—because you will suffer losses—but it will cure you of rebellion and restore you to the journey of purpose. Sarah suffered for causing her husband to take a detour. And Abraham suffered the loss of His son, Ishmael.

In Genesis 17:18 (KJV), Abraham tried to force Ishmael into God's purpose. *"And Abraham said unto God, O that Ishmael might live before thee!"* But God emphasized that the true heir would come from Sarah. In Genesis 21: 8-11, we see an incident that caused Abraham to lose his son, Ishmael. Not through death, but a divine purging... You will lose everything you got from your detour, and later on, it will come back to haunt you. Today, the children of the bondwoman are the greatest enemies of Israel, God's people. So, allow the will of God to prevail even as you journey towards the fulfillment of your purpose.

Call to Action

Share an experience where you've had to let go of a desire you once conceived for the sake of God's will for your life.

Prayers.

Father, in the name of Jesus, I thank You once again because You have a will for my life. I pray that You purge me of every and any desire that is not according to Your will. I know it can be painful, but I believe with Your Spirit I will overcome. Help me to rest only in Your purpose for my life. Deliver me from alternatives that will only lead me astray and help me align with You. In Jesus' name. Amen.

DAY 23
THE POTTER'S WHEEL

Scriptural Text: *"But now, O Lord, you are our Father, we are the clay, and You our Potter; and all of us are the work of Your hand."*
–Isaiah 64:8 NIV

Inspiring Commentary

We all desire and love the good things of life. However, suffering and trials aren't part of what we ever desire to we experience. We desire a relaxing ride through life with zero bumps or challenges on our paths. But the truth is that God's unique purpose shapes the work of God in our lives. And for the kind of person God wants you to be, there would be a necessary heat He must take you through. Yes, we all sometimes struggle with God turning up the heat of making on us, but we must trust the hand that makes us.

Isaiah 64:8 (KJV) says, *"But now, O Lord, you are our Father, we are the clay, and You our Potter; and all of us are the work of Your hand."* Think about this Scripture a little deeper. What we are (as believers) in the hand of God is clay--selfless and yielded beings. The beauty of hand-crafted pottery reflects the work and excellence of the potter. At first, the clay never looks admirable or unique--just a pile of dense, unattractive clay! Until the final touch of the potter, it's hard to project what the potter is up to.

So, trust the process, and a unique you will emerge out of God's creative wheel. What if Joseph had aborted the process of making by sleeping with Potiphar's wife? Or sleep remained in prison with no hope in the living God. Joseph went through the Potter's hand thoroughly formed and made into a unique character in the history of God's people. Willingness to go through the process makes you patient and enduring. You don't see anything you go through as a drowning sea but a momentary and light affliction. God makes every messy life by His mercy into great vessels.

In a class full of toddlers, there's a lot of hum and buzz. Their teachers are often exhausted but also delighted at the innocence of their little pupils. Imagine that in such a class, the teacher announces she will choose some of the kids to make a presentation before others. You can be sure that many tiny hands will be raised with cries of "pick me! pick me!"

When the King-Potter wants to choose the clay to make His vessels, there's no such excitement. There are two reasons for this. First, the clay isn't certain he or she will be picked because of the parameters of the manufacturer's selection. Second, clay is baked in the fire, an experience that neither looks nor feels excitement-worthy.

You might wonder, "I thought everyone is born with a purpose; what's this about being chosen?" Matthew 22:14 (KJV) provides the answer: *"For many are called, but few are chosen."* For instance, many Godly people lived in the Bible's time, but not everyone featured in the Scriptures. There were one hundred and twenty disciples in the upper room who received the promise of the Holy Ghost and tongues of fire, yet not all were chosen to appear in the book of Acts or the New Testament epistles. So, it's time to lay down and allow the Potter to do quick work of making you into that glorious vessel for the world to see.

Call to Action

How can you prepare yourself for the Potter's molding process?

____

____

____

____

____

Prayers

Father, in the name of Jesus, I thank You for your presence in my life. I lay down my all to Your wheel today, and I pray that You mold me to your desire. I am a lump of clay in Your hand, so I pray that You will create me afresh, bake me, and smoothen my rough edges so I can be all You have created me to be. I surrender all to You, withholding nothing. In Jesus' name. Amen.

DAY 24

STRETCH BEYOND YOUR LIMIT

Scriptural Text: *"My brethren, count it all joy when ye fall into divers temptations; knowing this, that the trying of your faith worketh patience. But let patience have her perfect work, that ye may be perfect and entire, wanting nothing."*

–James 1:2-4 KJV

Inspiring Commentary

The sun that melts the ice is the same that solidifies the clay. What distinguishes between both is inner strength and makeup. In life, what many go through and becomes stronger and settled is what others go through, broken and shattered. God will stretch you beyond your limits to be used greatly by God. Remaining in your comfort zone cripples you in destiny. *More* is the language of anyone who will make an impact and full delivery of His purpose in life.

Many today are experts in creating good wishes about the future they aren't actively preparing themselves for. Complacency is a thief of greatness. One character that always impresses and inspires me in Scripture, among others, is Apostle Paul. He so much understood the language of stretching beyond limits. He testified that even though everything he did was by the grace of God, he labored more than all the Apostles before him. This is impressive!

Today, hardly will you hear a seasoned sermon without hearing the name of Paul. He allowed God to stretch him for his purpose-that is the work of ministry. He left his comfort zone into a place of constant peril and trials. He experienced shipwreck, beatings, stoning, and imprisonment. But yet, he remained steadfast in following God's plan for his life. Another character that was stretched beyond the limit in the Old Testament was Job. He lost everything, but not his trust and confidence in God. This is the only way to walk in destiny and be fulfilled.

Instead of complaints in the season of pain and discomfort, learn from Job. He said I know my Redeemer lives. Sometimes, God uses people in your life to stretch you beyond the limit. It may just be your 'wicked boss,' who will never take anything less than excellent from you. Under such a person, you experience stretching. Always see God behind the scenes as He makes everything work together for your good.

Chapter 42 of the book of Job shows that he passed the test. But what kept him during the grievous testing period wasn't only the fact that he was pitch-perfect, but he also had an in-depth understanding of God's ways. He understood God was testing him. He said in Job 23:8-10 (NCV), *"If I go to the east, God is not there;* if *I go to the west, I do not see him. When he is at work in the north, I catch no sight of him; when he turns to the south, I cannot see him. But God knows the way that I take, and when he has tested me, I will come out like gold."*

Job knew that God was working amid the circumstance. God also used people. For instance, Jesus didn't crucify or flog Himself. Human beings did those things to Him. Yet, those were ordained circumstances for His glorification. May you not wriggle out circumstances orchestrated for your glory! Don't be offended by those who seem to be torn in your flesh.

God uses impatient people to teach us patience and wicked ones to teach us, love. He uses perilous situations to teach us faith. Every day,

God teaches us through our experiences. He works amid the circumstance. Therefore, it's good to pray, "Lord, teach me today, break me and mold me." You can't influence more in life by staying within your limit, it's time to stretch beyond where you are now.

Call to Action

Have you been given a responsibility before that demanded that you go out of your comfort zone? What was your response?

____

____

____

____

____

Prayer

Father, in the name of Jesus, I thank You for Your Word today. I know I have what it takes to be all You have created me to be. So I pray that You stretch me in preparation for what lies ahead. You are all-knowing, so I submit to You to give me the inner propensity, the faith and the spiritual stamina to face the challenges that lie ahead and still fulfill my purpose. In Jesus' name. Amen.

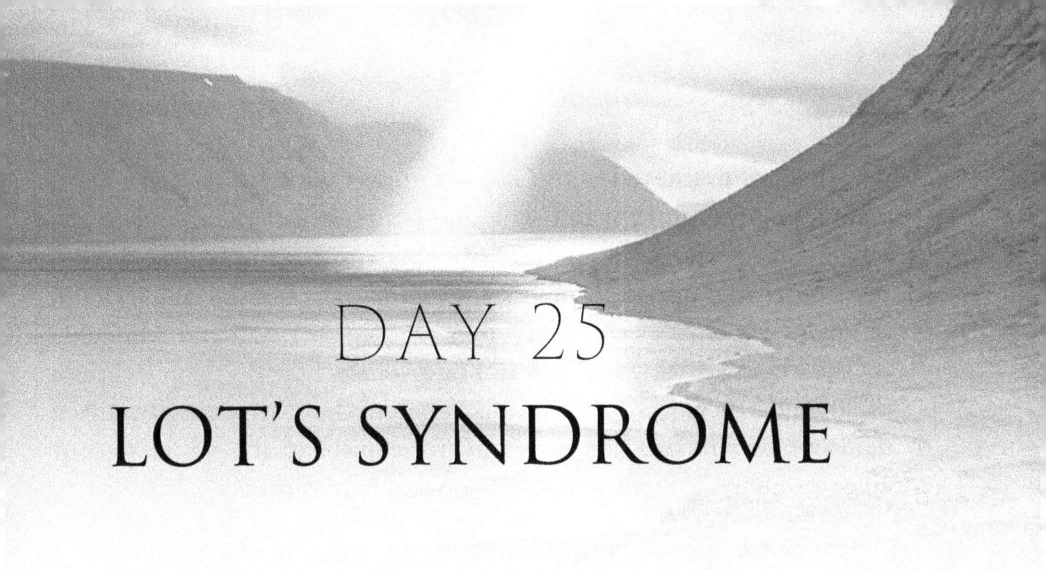

DAY 25
LOT'S SYNDROME

Scriptural Text: "*While we look not at the things which are seen, but at the things which are not seen: for the things which are seen are temporal; but the things which are not seen are eternal.***"**

–2 Corinthians 4:18 KJV

Inspiring Commentary

As humans, we are more persuaded to pursue what we see than stay with God's unseen, His promises. We never see beyond our nose into the grand plans of God for our lives. Many's pursuits in life are defined by the mundane. What they see with their physical eyes has superimposed God's milk and honey land for them. What is Lot's syndrome? Lot's syndrome is walking by sight. Making decisions shaped by what is seen, even if it will take you into a corrupt territory and lifestyle. God blesses His children, but not at the expense of their divine election.

Men with this syndrome will do anything to pursue their desire even if God is not pleased. They care less about God in their decisions. God's will is only a weak alternative. In fact, God isn't any close to their minds when it comes to making big decisions! Friend, you'll devise alien means to God's kingdom if you walk and live by sight. That's a dead-end in walking in divine purpose! It takes faith to walk with God! If God is Spirit and He's the Giver of purpose, only men of faith can walk into the heights of His counsel for their lives.

Abraham journeyed with God into uncertainties. He never knew what to expect but kept following the God that called him out of the Ur of Chaldeans. While the life of Abraham became a generational blessing, by the instrumentality of his faith-walk, Lot became a victim of his carnal choices. Not everything that looks good and admirable is God's counsel for your destiny. For instance, how do people choose their life partners today? While it isn't bad to desire or want a beautiful damsel for a wife or a handsome guy for a husband, it is wrong to start and stop there. You must go beyond what man can see.

Just as we have the physical eyes to direct us on our path, we also have our spiritual eyes to see things beyond the physical. Indeed, the purposes of God are not always communicated in the physical but through the Spirit. The Bible says in 1 Corinthians 2:9-11 (KJV), "But, as it is written, *"What no eye has seen, nor ear heard, nor the heart of man imagined, what God has prepared for those who love Him"— these things God has revealed to us through the Spirit. For the Spirit searches everything, even the depths of God. For who knows a person's thoughts except the spirit of that person, which is in him? So also no one comprehends the thoughts of God except the Spirit of God."*

This shows that God's purposes are communicated through the Spirit. His plan is revealed to us by the help of the Holy Spirit, so you need an active spiritual vision to see what God has written concerning you and walk in the reality of it. This, I believe, is the missing link for most people. As crucial as physical sight is in an individual's life, the absence of spiritual sight can totally render physical vision useless.

However, you needed to visualize the promise. God understood the power of sight, and so He took Abraham through a spiritual sight therapy so he could see the extent of what lies ahead of him. The Bible says in Genesis 13:12-17 (NLT), *"So Abram settled in the land of Canaan, and Lot moved his tents to a place near Sodom and settled among the cities of the plain. But the people of this area were extremely wicked and constantly sinned against the Lord. After Lot had gone, the Lord said to Abram, "Look as far as you can see in every direction—north and south, east and west. I am giving all this land, as far as you can see, to you and your descendants as a permanent possession. And I will give you so many descendants that, like the dust of the earth, they can-*

not be counted! Go and walk through the land in every direction, for I am giving it to you." So, open your spiritual eyes and see beyond what your physical sight can access regarding your purpose. You have a glorious assignment which cannot be achieved by mundane expectations.

Call to Action

Have you ever taken a step in the past that later cost you dearly? How did you find your footing again?

____

____

____

____

____

Prayers

Father, in the name of Jesus, I thank You for the ability to have spiritual sight. I thank You for the gift of Your Holy Spirit in my life. I pray that You will open my spiritual sight today. I ask for the grace not to be deceived like Lot into going after what I can see around me. I pray that my inner eyes be open always to Your purpose for my life. In Jesus' name. Amen.

DAY 26
GOD'S HABITATION

Scriptural Text: *"In whom ye also are builded together for a habitation of God through the Spirit."*

–Ephesians 2:22 KJV

Inspiring Commentary

Men build houses according to their taste and what would like to do with them. In the same vein, God builds with His counsel in view. And whatever God cannot live in, He will not build. In the Old Testament, God permitted Solomon to build a temple-a holy habitation so He could dwell. This was a pressing desire of David, his father. David, the great psalmist, seems to have a unique reverence and experience of God's presence growing up. He was alone at the backside of the desert, where he kept his father's flock.

God's presence became a priceless commodity to David, and the building of habitation for God grew in his heart. Even though Solomon fulfilled the long desire of his father by building a temple, God wanted something more personal and individualistic. He needed a resting place in the heart of men, not just some physical Tabernacle. God's habitat has always been within man. That's the major purpose of creating the body. Your body was fashioned to host God, and from there, He perpetuates His will.

Ephesians 2:22 says, *"In whom ye also are builded together for a habitation of God through the Spirit."* The word habitation in this verse denotes a dwelling place or a permanent residence of God. God builds men so He could find a resting/dwelling place in them. Until God's Spirit finds a home in you, to receive His counsel will be impossible. This is why an unbeliever cannot do or fulfill God's mandate and assignment. He can't even know it! Simply put, what fills a man is what flows through him.

The Bible says in a great house, there are many vessels (2 Timothy 2:20-22). Yes, God loves to create vessels of various shapes, sizes, and worth for His use. His house is great. There's a profound lesson here. You can't become a vessel until you become a member of God's house. This has two implications. You either become a part of a great man's house through birth or service. So, you're either the man's child or his servant. Glory to God; anyone in Christ is a child of God, but then, even as children, we are called to God's service. Therefore, although we are sons (children of God), we yield ourselves to God to serve His purposes.

In Romans 1:1 (KJV) Paul introduced himself as, *"a servant of Jesus Christ, called to be an apostle, separated unto the gospel of God."* This implies that serving God and His interest in the earth is a capital indicator of serving His purpose for our lives. Allow the Holy Spirit to fill your heart richly, and through His awesome presence, He begins to communicate His golden will to your spirit.

Call to Action

How committed are you in serving God?

____

____

____

____

____

Prayer

Father, in the name of Jesus, I pray that You dwell in my life afresh today. I ask that You show me the path and the way of life. I pray that You keep me committed to serving You and Your purpose anywhere I find myself. Let my life be habitable by You. In Jesus' name. Amen.

DAY 27

SPYING THE GIANTS

Scriptural Text: *"After we went through Ammon, the LORD told us: Israel, pack up your possessions, take down your tents, and cross the Arnon River gorge. The territory of the Amorite King Sihon of Heshbon lies on the other side of the river, but I now give you his land. So attack and take it!"*

–Deuteronomy 2:24 CEV

Inspiring Commentary

Most of the time, we get scared and chicken out of a profession or field because of the perceived giants there. Unfortunately, not many people have the right attitude and courage to get into a market/field, grow in/with the market, and make striking accomplishments and impact. This isn't because they have no strength or energy to birth something unique and unusual; it's simply that every field has giants who have written their names with pearls of gold and have raised the bar of excellence that many may not dear to beat.

While it is normal for the nervous to pull out, what should be the propensity of the Christian in their field of influence? First, identify the giants in your field and learn from them. This is a necessary addition to your progress and growth in destiny. Have you ever thought of the reason Jesus asked the teachers and rulers of His day critical questions at the age of 12? He was spying on the giants! Even though with a unique calling and purpose, He spied for the best in His field and understood the best way to launch into His father's business.

He tested those already in the business of souls in His days before diving in. He did that so early, such that, at the age of thirty, He already became an authority in His field. He came fully prepared for the contest of ministry in such a way that brings glory and honour like never! When you're ignorant of your competitors, you fall short in preparation. All the tools you employ must match the best practice of your field. And this is only possible by careful spying out on the giants in your promised land of destiny and assignment.

Secondly, you must have a well-established strategy to raise the bar. No scientist becomes great by disposing off prior discoveries and theories in his field. They only thrive as they build on the glories of past scientific research, discoveries, and theories. After marking the giants, develop your next action plan for achieving a better feat. Yes, God promised you a land flowing with milk and honey, but you must recognize early that there are giants there. Spy them out!

Numbers 13:17-20 (KJV) says, *"And Moses sent them to spy out the land of Canaan, and said unto them, Get you up this way southward, and go up into the mountain: And see the land, what it is; and the people that dwelleth therein, whether they be strong or weak, few or many;"* When you know who God wants you to be, decide to be the best and succeed at the highest level. To do this, you need to study how others with the same purpose became successful. But don't just look out for anyone making money or impact; go for the giants. Some people are one of a kind, the best in their field, follow those people. Someone said, "Aim for the moon, if you miss, you'll land among the stars."[19] Desire to be among the stars.

How do you follow the best? Study them. This involves diligent research, reading books, studying their patterns and strategies, adjusting to certain lifestyles, etc. For instance, if you are called to be a writer and desire to be one of the best, you must study the books of great writers. Your purpose is to be set on a hill where your purpose can't be hidden, so go for it.

Call to Action

What aspect of life are you struggling to rise to the top?

____

____

____

____

____

Do you have anyone in your field you are studying? If no, it's time to locate one.

____

____

____

____

____

Prayer

Father, in the name of Jesus, I thank You for the revelation of Your Word today. I pray that You give me a lion heart so I can take over and rule in my field. I will no longer give in to pressures and opposition. Distractions will no longer carry me away. I pray that You will strengthen me to rise above the sky in honor of Your name. In Jesus' name. Amen.

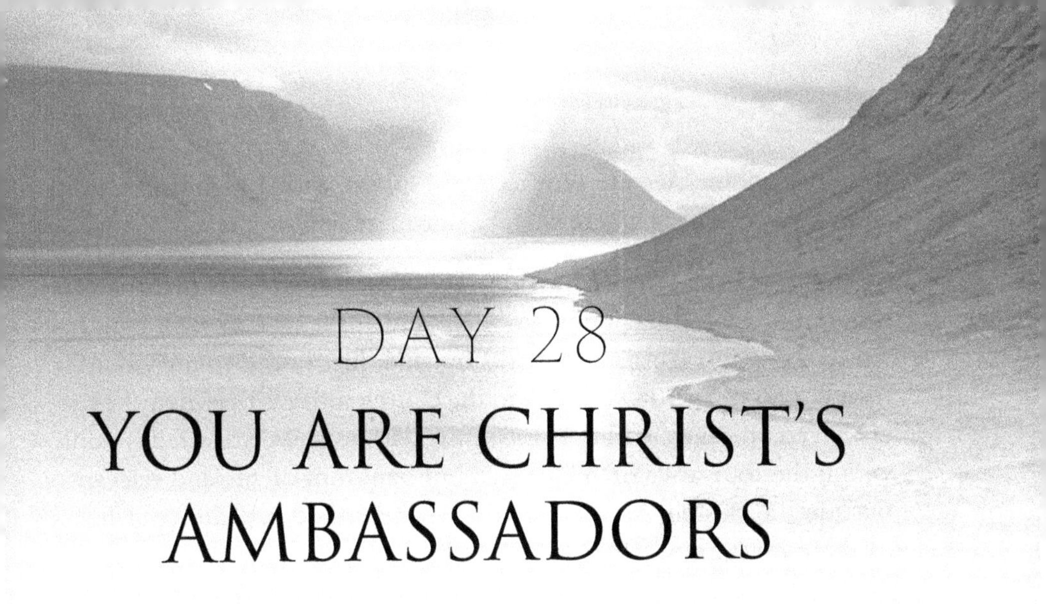

DAY 28

YOU ARE CHRIST'S AMBASSADORS

Scriptural Text: *“Now then we are ambassadors for Christ, as though God did beseech you by us: we pray you in Christ's stead, be ye reconciled to God.”*

–2 Corinthians 5:20 KJV

Inspiring Commentary

An ambassador is a diplomat. One who represents the highest authority of their homeland in another country. They work in another country but retain the citizenship of their home country. The operations and guidelines of the ambassador are strictly guided by the country he represents. Even though they are living in a host nation, they serve their home nation and affect national relations between the two countries. Feedback and connectivity with the home country are vital for an ambassador.

More so, the ambassador isn't there for his interest. He represents and must push for the wellness of his home country. Isn't this what God demands from every believer on earth? Aren't we supposed to live exactly as ambassadors while we are here? The text above says, “You are an ambassador for Christ. Even though it doesn't look fashionable to say anymore in our highly enlightened society, this world is not our home! We are sent to every sphere with a high expectation from heaven. That's where we take our marching orders.

However, one remarkable thing about ambassadors is that they are sent out of their domain into another land as the face of their country. An Ambassador labors and works outside their home country but for their country. One tragic reality in the church today is that many believers haven't been trained to shine in the darkness. We are effective only within the four walls of the church but bankrupt of life and relevance outside the church. Meanwhile, that's where God ordained our lights to shine for Him.

When you take a look at God's original intent for creation, you will find at the heart of it a desire to illuminate the whole earth with the life of God. Man's making is a precursor for the representative role they were created to perform. It was to the end that the rule of God be extended to the earth that we were created in God's image.

God has a purpose for you beyond the four walls of the church. Yes, you have an assignment in God's house, but beyond the house of God, you have a purpose in the marketplace. You weren't called to remain in the house of God forever in terms of geographical location but to be a carrier of God's presence. His purpose for your life is far beyond the two or three hours you spend on Sunday or Bible study sessions with the brethren, your purpose will be fulfilled out there beyond the church. This is one truth most Christians don't want to admit.

In Luke 4, the Bible says Jesus found where it was written concerning Him; that is, He discovered His purpose in the church among the brethren. But in Acts 10, we saw where He fulfilled that purpose-on the street, in the marketplace, among tax collectors, by the sea-side with the fishers. This is a classic example of what God has called us into.

Jesus could have remained in the synagogue after He discovered His purpose. He knew His purpose was to preach the kingdom to the people, yet He didn't sit back down in the synagogue, wearing robes and accepting offerings. He harnessed the marketplace. The Father gave Jesus grace without measure, and it was manifested on the street because those are the people He was sent to. Simply put, like Jesus, the fulfillment of your purpose is out there, not in here. So, go out and represent Christ today.

Call to Action

Has God shown you the people He has sent you to? If not, it's time to locate where you are ordained to shine.

____

____

____

____

____

Prayer

Father, in the name of Jesus, I thank You for making me into an Ambassador. I pray that You help me to locate where You have assigned me to shine as a light You have made me to be. I pray that You give me the wisdom and boldness to stand for truth beyond the church walls. I pray that through the help of the Holy Spirit, I will shine brighter through the darkness in the world. In Jesus' name. Amen.

DAY 29

A LEAP INTO THE FUTURE

Scriptural Text: *"And the LORD said unto Abram, after that Lot was separated from him, Lift up now thine eyes, and look from the place where thou art northward, and southward, and eastward, and westward: For all the land which thou seest, to thee will I give it, and to thy seed forever."*
–Genesis 13:14-15 KJV

Inspiring Commentary

Jesus died more than two thousand years ago in Jerusalem with few disciples. It doesn't look reasonable, but He lived for the glory set before Him. Everything and everyone in hell was against the purpose of Christ on earth, but He never yielded to the pressure and the pain His ministry attracted; rather, He leapt into the future of His sacrifices and commitments to the Father's purpose and call. How far and how well we see into the future will set the tone for how well we live today.

To live without a glimpse into the future is to walk the path of purpose without a trans-generational outlook and preparedness. The Bible says about Jesus, *"Looking unto Jesus the Author and Finisher of our faith; who for the joy that was set before Him endured the cross, despising the shame, and is set down at the right hand of the throne of God. For consider Him that endured such contradiction of sinners against Himself, lest ye be wearied and faint in your minds."* (Hebrews 12:2-3 KJV)

What Jesus saw in His future infused into Him the ability and courage to make hard sacrifices. He saw the glory at the end of the journey so He could endure the process and embrace His purpose. Think about it for a moment. Why do people let go at the slightest sense of challenges? Why do people relax once it doesn't look profitable at the moment? No trans-generational mentality—that's why! Jesus never lived for now. He saw into more than two thousand years after His death, and to endure the cross became a light affliction that cannot be compared with the glory that comes after. To survive the storms wrapped around your purpose, you must leap into the future of it and catch a glimpse of its beautiful end!

It's important to understand that God's purpose for your life doesn't end with you or your immediate family. He wants to affect your children and their children. He commits purposes to generations. An understanding of this truth will make you pay attention to your purpose and align on time and accordingly. It will interest you to know that some people's purpose is hinged on yours.

Let's view it this way. In a typical textile manufacturing company, we have staff working in different departments of the organization. Some are in charge of cutting the cloth; others will sew the pieces together based on the measurement; some others will add buttons or zip to the close; another session will whip the cloth to remove excess threads, and then another session will iron the cloth.

By implication, the finished product of one department is the raw material of another. In other words, the work in a department depends on the outcome of another department, and the cycle continues. In the same vein, some people may not maximize or fulfill their purpose if you lay yours aside. Just imagine that Jesus came to the world and remained a carpenter rather than accepting responsibility for His purpose; how will Peter become an Apostle? How will he embody such a dimension of supernatural power that made his shadow heal the sick? Friend, raise your head beyond yourself and follow through with God.

See the end of the journey and get excited as God takes you one step at a time.

Call to Action

Have you discovered the lives and destinies that are attached to your purpose?

____

____

____

____

____

Prayer

Father, in the name of Jesus, thank You for not giving me a mediocre purpose. I now know that I am not all to myself. My purpose is not just about me and what I can be. I pray that You will help me to maintain a trans-generational mindset even as I seek to fulfill my purpose. I pray that You will give me the stamina to hold fast to what You have committed into my hand so others may rejoice. In Jesus' name. Amen.

DAY 30

HEAVEN ON EARTH

Scriptural Text: *"After this manner therefore pray ye: Our Father which art in heaven, Hallowed be Thy name. Thy kingdom come. Thy will be done in earth, as it is in heaven."*

–Matthew 6:9-10 KJV

Inspiring Commentary

Think about God ruling the government, media world, fashion world, and the business world today. What peace and bliss the world would walk in and experience. Why is heaven peaceful and glorious? It runs by the will of the Father. Everything in heaven lives and moves at the instance of God's commands. Angels are beings fashioned to obey God's instructions and bedding. Hence, obedience to God's counsel and will is what makes for the experience of peace in heaven.

The desire of God isn't that this world is full of atrocities and evil. He wants a place where His will can be perpetuated and established. But if this will happen, God must first win the heart of men and reign in their hearts. It is when the rule of God prospers in a heart that it effortlessly pervades his space and territory. So that if you make it a must to know and obey God's will, God wins in your life and by extension, your family. It grows that way into society. In a nutshell, only conquered men can conquer their sphere of influence for God.

Corruption increases upon the earth when satan is enthroned in the heart of men. The rule of darkness in a life births an opposing lifestyle and purpose to God. The way the believer lives must constantly say one thing: Thy will be done in my life as it is in heaven. God's kingdom must be prime in our engagements anywhere we flourish as Christians. Know God's will, live God's will, and enforce God's will anywhere you find yourself! Start from your Jerusalem to the uttermost part of your world.

God desires that the world become the kingdom of God and His Christ, which is only possible if His children are working in His purpose for their lives. Jesus said in Hebrews 10:7 (KJV), *"Then said I, Lo, I come (in the volume of the book it is written of me,) to do thy will, O God."* Jesus lived and preached about the kingdom because His life was wrapped around doing the will of the Father.

The Bible says in Luke chapter 4 of an occasion when, after preaching and healing on the Sabbath day, Jesus rose the next morning to depart to a solitary place as His custom was, but the crowd found Him and appealed to Him to stay. But He responded in Luke 4:43, *"But He said to them, "I must preach the good news of the kingdom of God to the other towns as well; for I was sent for this purpose."* This goes to show that a number of times God is counting on you to show forth the mysteries of the kingdom but it begins with you discovering and responding to your purpose.

God's kingdom is restored to the earth anytime someone says yes to Jesus. Anytime someone accepts the challenge of fulfilling God's purpose for them. The Excellency of God is only manifested in earthen vessels. Have you said yes to this golden call?

Call to Action

What is your understanding of this statement, "Thy kingdom come?"

____

____

____

____

____

Prayer

Father, in the name of Jesus, I thank You for the reality of the kingdom of God in my life. I pray that You help me to align with kingdom principles and ways. I pray that You will give me the grace to always say yes to Your will and bring to bear the reality of the kingdom in my generation. In Jesus' name. Amen.

ABOUT THE AUTHOR

Apostle L'Tanya C. Perry, MDiv.

Apostle L'Tanya C. Perry, MDiv. is a dynamic and visionary leader whose passion for raising Godly leaders is worthy of note. She is the senior pastor and founder of New Beginnings Worship Center in Hudson, North Carolina, where she has raised a people of influence for the past 14 years. While concurrently founding New Beginnings Worship Center, she also launched TAP-Training with Apostle Perry, available on Facebook Live and other social media platforms.

With a burning desire to become relevant, not just to the kingdom but also to the society, she established a firm, Perry's Accounting and Tax Mobile Services.

The firm was founded 18 years ago and still runs to date. Craving excellence in all she does, she has been compelled to pursue a Ph.D. in Business Administration, specializing in Organizational Leadership. She has obtained her Master in Divinity, Bachelor of Science in Business Administration, and Associate of Art in Biblical Studies.

She's happily married to Kelvin D. Perry, Sr. They have two children, Alexus and KJ.

For more information, visit the websites **ltanyaperry.org**, **ltanyaperry.com, mytap.org** or subscribe to our Facebook Group: **TAP.**

ENDNOTES

[1] DINARRECAPS8. "The Billionaire Who Wanted to Die Broke . . . Is Now Officially Broke." Dinar Recaps. Dinar Recaps, September 25, 2020. https://dinarrecaps.com/our-blog/the-billionaire-who-wanted-to-die-broke-is-now-officially-broke.

[2] DINARRECAPS8.

[3] Vince Lombardi. AZQuotes.com, Wind and Fly LTD, 2022. https://www.azquotes.com/quote/178117, accessed July 31, 2022.

[4] DINARRECAPS8.

[5] "Myles Munroe Quotes about Purpose: A-Z Quotes." A. Accessed July 30, 2022. https://www.azquotes.com/author/19226-Myles_Munroe/tag/purpose.

[6] "Purpose Definition and Meaning: Collins English Dictionary." Purpose definition and meaning | Collins English Dictionary. HarperCollins Publishers Ltd. Accessed July 30, 2022. https://www.collinsdictionary.com/dictionary/english/purpose.

[7] "A Quote from Understanding the Purpose and Power of Woman." Goodreads. Goodreads. Accessed July 30, 2022. https://www.goodreads.com/quotes/688275-when-purpose-is-not-known-abuse-is-inevitable.

[8] Gordon, Sherri. "What Are the Five Love Languages?" Verywell Mind. Verywell Mind, January 24, 2022. https://www.verywellmind.com/can-the-five-love-languages-help-your-relationship-4783538.

[9] Ritchie, Hannah, and Max Roser. "Drug Use." Our World in Data, December 5, 2019. https://ourworldindata.org/drug-use.

[10] "Myles Munroe Quotes about Purpose: A-Z Quotes." A. Accessed July 30, 2022. https://www.azquotes.com/author/19226-Myles_Munroe/tag/purpose.

[11] "You Are Not an Accident." You Are Not an Accident - Daily Devotion | CBN.com. Accessed July 30, 2022. https://www.cbn.com/spirituallife/Devotions/warren_noaccident0301.aspx.

[12] "It Is Not the Strongest of the Species That Survives but the Most Adaptable – Quote Investigator." Google. Google. Accessed July 30, 2022. https://www.google.com/amp/s/quoteinvestigator.com/2014/05/04/adapt/amp/.

[13] "Conduit Definition & Meaning." Merriam-Webster. Merriam-Webster. Accessed July 30, 2022. https://www.merriam-webster.com/dictionary/conduit.

[14] "Sermons, Outlines, Illustrations, and Preaching Ideas." Trending Free Sermon Outlines & Illustrations for Preaching Ideas. Accessed July 30, 2022. https://www.sermonsearch.com/sermon-outlines/19763/abraham-the-wonderful-journey-of-faith/.

[15] "Trigger Definition & Meaning." Dictionary.com. Dictionary.com. Accessed July 30, 2022. https://www.dictionary.com/browse/trigger.

[16] "TRIGGER ." Google search. Google. Accessed August 8, 2022. https://www.google.com/search?q=TRIGGER&rlz=1C1CHBF_enUS918US918&oq=TRIGGER&aqs=chrome..69i57j0i131i433i512j46i131i433i512j0i131i433i51212j46i433i512j0i131i433i512j69i60.11040j0j7&sourceid=chrome&ie=UTF-8.

[17] "Hagiazo Meaning in Bible - New Testament Greek Lexicon - New American Standard." biblestudytools.com. Accessed July 30, 2022. http://www.biblestudytools.com/lexicons/greek/nas/hagiazo.html.

[18] By. "How Deep Do You Have to Dig to Find Gold?" Yes Dirt, September 13, 2021. https://yesdirt.com/how-deep-do-you-have-to-dig-to-find-gold/.

[19] Unknown. Running Hamburg, January 1, 1970. https://runninghamburg.blogspot.com/.

Printed in the USA
CPSIA information can be obtained
at www.ICGtesting.com
LVHW021455060124
768255LV00005B/267

9 781957 052786